The Great American Cookbook

Exploring the Flavorful World of American Cuisine

by - Joris Birt

© 2023 Joris Birt. All rights reserved.

....

Licensing Notice

Kindly refrain from duplicating this book in any form, whether printed or electronic, and from selling, publishing, disseminating, or distributing it. Only those who have received express written consent from the author may engage in such activities.

This book has been meticulously crafted by the author, taking all possible precautions to ensure the content is both accurate and helpful. Nevertheless, it is essential for readers to exercise caution in their actions. Should any unfavorable outcomes arise as a result of the reader's actions, please be advised that the author cannot be held responsible.

••••••••••••••••••••••••••••••••

Table of Contents

Introduction 5

Common Ingredients 8

   1. Skillet Chicken Pot Pie 10

   1. New England Clam Chowder 12

   2. Barbecue Meatloaf 15

   3. Apricot Ricotta Bagels 17

   4. Deviled Eggs 19

   5. Classic Oven Fried Chicken 21

   6. Spinach and Artichoke Dip 23

   7. Barbecue Pulled Chicken Sandwiches 25

   8. Easy Fried Chicken 28

   9. Texas Beef Brisket 30

   10. Apple Spiced Pork Chops with Raisins 32

   11. Cheeseburger and Bacon Pie 35

   12. Fried Chicken Waffles 38

   13. Kale Slaw with Hazelnut Dressing 41

   14. Sriracha and Cheddar Burgers 44

   15. Creamy Potato Salad 46

16. Gooey Mac and Cheese 48

17. Chicken Chimichangas 50

18. Chicken Noodle Soup 53

19. Tuna Noodle Casserole 55

20. Apple Pecan Chicken Salad 57

21. Twice Baked Potatoes 59

22. Southern Buttermilk Cornbread 61

23. Oklahoma Beef Brisket 63

24. New Mexican Fish Tacos 65

25. Buffalo Chicken Pizza 68

26. Blueberry Cobbler 70

27. White Sheet Cake 72

28. Fudgy Chocolate Brownies 75

29. Easy Apple Pie 77

Conclusion 79

Wish You the Best 80

Introduction

American cuisine is known for its diverse and eclectic flavors, reflecting the melting pot of cultures that make up the United States. From burgers and hotdogs to BBQ and apple pie, American food is as diverse as its people.

The origins of American food can be traced back to the Native American tribes who originally inhabited the land. Corn, beans, and squash were staples in their diets, and these ingredients remain a significant part of traditional American cuisine today. With the arrival of European settlers, new culinary influences were introduced, leading to the blending of traditional ingredients with European cooking techniques.

American cuisine has been greatly influenced by the immigrants who came to the country and brought their culinary traditions with them. The Italians, for example, introduced pizza and pasta, which are now widely enjoyed across the nation. Mexican immigrants popularized dishes like tacos, nachos, and burritos, which have become an integral part of American cuisine.

Fast food is another significant aspect of American food culture. The fast-food industry was pioneered in America, and it has spread throughout the world, with chains like McDonald's and KFC becoming global icons. Burgers, hotdogs, French fries, and milkshakes have become emblematic of American eating habits, representing the convenience and speed of modern life.

In recent years, there has been a growing emphasis on health-conscious eating and locally sourced ingredients in American cuisine. Farm-to-table restaurants and organic food movements have gained popularity, highlighting the importance of sustainability, fresh flavors, and supporting local farmers. This shift reflects a desire for healthier and more environmentally friendly choices, making American food more diverse and inclusive.

The United States is also known for its regional cuisine, each area having its own specialties and flavors. In the South, for example, BBQ is a beloved tradition, with variations like Memphis, Texas, and Carolina styles, showcasing different meat cuts and sauce preferences. The East Coast is famous for its seafood, with dishes like clam chowder and lobster rolls. The Midwest is known for hearty meals like casseroles and meat-based dishes, while the West Coast is associated with the farm-to-table movement and fusion cuisine.

Popular American desserts, too, are noteworthy for their indulgence and creativity. Apple pie, a classic American dish, has a long history of being associated with American culture, symbolizing patriotism and home-cooked comfort. Other beloved desserts include chocolate chip cookies, brownies, and the iconic American birthday cake.

American food is also heavily influenced by its industrialization and mass production. Convenience foods, frozen dinners, and canned products have become part of many American households, providing quick and easy meal options. However, there has been a growing movement to return to homemade meals and fresh ingredients, as people seek healthier and more authentic culinary experiences.

Common Ingredients

In American cuisine, you'll find a wide range of common ingredients that are frequently used to create the delicious and diverse dishes. Here are some staple ingredients you'll often come across in American recipes:

1. Meat: Beef, chicken, pork, and turkey are commonly used in a variety of dishes, from burgers and barbecue to stews and roasts.
2. Potatoes: Versatile and beloved, potatoes are used in various forms such as mashed potatoes, fries, hash browns, and potato salads.
3. Tomatoes: Whether in the form of fresh tomatoes, canned tomatoes, or tomato sauces, tomatoes play a key role in many dishes like pasta sauces, chili, and soups.
4. Corn: Corn is a staple ingredient in American cuisine and appears in dishes like cornbread, grits, and succotash.
5. Wheat Flour: Flour is used for making bread, biscuits, cakes, and other baked goods that are integral to American cooking.
6. Cheese: A favorite ingredient, cheese is used in everything from cheeseburgers and grilled cheese sandwiches to pizza and macaroni and cheese.
7. Eggs: Eggs are a crucial component in various recipes, such as breakfast dishes, baked goods, and salads.
8. Beans: Whether black beans, pinto beans, or kidney beans, they're featured in dishes like chili, burritos, and salads.
9. Onions: Onions add depth and flavor to many recipes, from sautéed vegetables to soups and stews.
10. Bell Peppers: Colorful bell peppers are commonly used in salads, stir-fries, and fajitas.
11. Bacon: A beloved addition for its smoky flavor, bacon is often incorporated into dishes like burgers, salads, and breakfast items.
12. Butter: A key ingredient for adding richness and flavor to a wide range of recipes, from savory to sweet.

13. Barbecue Sauce: A quintessential American condiment used for marinating and glazing meats in barbecue dishes.
14. Mustard: Often used as a condiment for sandwiches and hot dogs, as well as in dressings and sauces.
15. Mayonnaise: A common base for salads, dressings, and sandwich spreads.
16. Pickles: A tangy and crunchy addition to sandwiches, burgers, and relish trays.
17. Hot Sauce: For those who crave heat, hot sauce is added to dishes to spice them up.
18. Maple Syrup: A natural sweetener used to drizzle over pancakes, waffles, and French toast.

These ingredients represent just a glimpse of the diverse and flavorful world of American cuisine, showcasing the fusion of flavors and cultural influences that make it so unique.

1. Skillet Chicken Pot Pie

Chicken pot pie is another American staple and is typically made in the Southern region of the country. This dish is an easier take on a complicated dish that is perfect for the entire family.

Serving Size: 6

Cooking Time: 25 minutes

Ingredients:

- 8 pound rotisserie chicken, shredded
- 14 ounce can of mixed vegetables
- 14 ounce can of cream of chicken soup
- Dash of salt and black pepper
- 1 bunch of parsley, chopped
- 1 (10-ounce) container of buttermilk biscuits

Instructions:

Heat the oven to 425 deg. F. Grease a huge cast iron skillet with butter or cooking spray.

In a large bowl, add in the shredded rotisserie chicken and the drained can of mixed vegetables. Stir well to mix.

Add in the cream of chicken soup. Season using a dash of salt and black pepper. Stir again.

Pour the chicken mixture into the greased skillet. Top off with the buttermilk biscuits.

Place into the oven to bake for 20 minutes at 425 degrees F.

Remove and garnish with the chopped parsley. Serve.

1. New England Clam Chowder

This is the perfect dish for you to make whenever you are feeling under the weather. For the best results, be sure to serve this dish with freshly baked bread.

Serving Size: 4 to 6

Cooking Time: 25 minutes

Ingredients:

- 2 tablespoons of unsalted butter
- 1 onion, chopped
- 2 stalks of celery, cut into quarters
- 3 tablespoons of all-purpose flour
- 2 cups of chicken stock
- 2 (10-ounce) cans of clams, chopped
- 1 cup of heavy cream
- 2 bay leaves
- 1 pound of Idaho potatoes, cut into small cubes
- Dash of salt and black pepper
- For the croutons:
- 2 to 3 tablespoons of unsalted butter
- ½ of a baguette, cut into small cubes
- 3 tablespoons of flat leaf parsley, chopped
- Dash of salt and black pepper

Instructions:

Place a large pot over medium to high heat. Add in the butter then once melted, add in the chopped onion and celery quarters. Stir well to mix then cook for 5 minutes or until soft.

Add in the all-purpose flour and toss to coat.

Add in the chicken stock, clam juice, heavy whipping cream, bay leaves and Idaho potatoes. Stir well to mix.

Simmer the mixture then reduce the heat to low. Cook for 20 minutes or until the potatoes are soft.

Add in the clams and season with a dash of salt and black pepper. Cook for another 2 to 3 minutes.

In a separate large skillet, add in the remaining butter. Once melted, add in the bread cubes. Cook for 5 minutes or until toasted. Add in the chopped parsley and season with a dash of salt and black pepper.

Serve the clam chowder with the croutons.

2. Barbecue Meatloaf

If there is one thing many Americans love, it is food smothered in barbecue sauce. This is another delicious barbecued dish that is hard to resist.

Serving Size: 4

Cooking Time: 50 minutes

Ingredients:

- 1 pound of 90% ground lean beef
- ½ cup of panko breadcrumbs
- 1 tablespoon + 2 teaspoons of Worcestershire sauce
- 1 tablespoon of Dijon mustard
- 4 tablespoons of smoky barbecue sauce
- 1 tablespoon of honey
- ½ teaspoon of salt
- ½ teaspoon of black pepper

Instructions:

Preheat the oven to 350 degrees F.

In a large bowl, add in the lean beef, panko breadcrumbs, Worcestershire sauce, Dijon mustard and barbecue sauce. Season using a dash of salt and black pepper. Stir well to mix.

Shape the mixture into a large log. Place into a large baking dish.

In your small bowl, add in 1 tablespoon of the barbecue sauce, 2 teaspoons of the Worcestershire sauce and the honey. Whisk until smooth in consistency.

Pour the mixture over the meatloaf.

Bring into the oven to bake for 45 minutes.

Remove and serve.

3. Apricot Ricotta Bagels

These delicious bagels are the perfect lazy-day breakfast option. This recipe is good with other stone fruits like peaches, nectarines, or plums.

Serving Size: 2

Cooking Time: 5 to 10 minutes

Ingredients:

- 1 cup low-fat ricotta cheese
- 1 tablespoon honey
- 1/2 teaspoon ground cinnamon
- 1/2 teaspoon vanilla extract
- 2 bagels of choice, sliced in half
- 4 fresh apricots, thinly sliced
- 1/4 cup coarsely chopped pistachios

Instructions:

Combine the ricotta, honey, cinnamon and vanilla. Toast the bagel halves.

Spread the cheese mixture on the toasted bagels, and top with apricot slices and pistachios.

Enjoy!

4. Deviled Eggs

This recipe for classic devilled eggs is easy to prepare and something the whole family is sure to enjoy. Try it out at your next dinner party as an appetizer or hors d'oeuvre.

Serving Size: 12

Cooking Time: 15 minutes

Ingredients:

- 6 large eggs
- Water, as needed
- ¼ cup mayonnaise
- ½ teaspoon dry mustard powder
- Salt and pepper to taste
- Paprika, to serve (qty. as desired(

Instructions:

Bring the eggs in a saucepan then add enough cold water to cover them by 1".

Boil the water then cover and remove from heat.

Set aside for 8 to 10 minutes then drain and run cool water over them.

Peel the eggs then cut them in half lengthwise.

Remove the yolks to a bowl and stir in the mayonnaise, mustard, salt and pepper.

Spoon the filling back into the eggs and sprinkle with paprika to serve.

5. Classic Oven Fried Chicken

This classic fried chicken recipe is perfect for lunch or dinner. Juicy on the inside and made with a breaded, crunchy outside, make sure to serve this dish with fresh mashed potatoes for the tastiest results.

Serving Size: 8

Cooking Time: 40 minutes

Ingredients:

- 2 (6-ounce each) chicken breasts, boneless and skinless
- 2 ½ cup of all-purpose flour
- 1 teaspoon of salt
- 1 teaspoon of black pepper
- 1 teaspoon of Hungarian paprika
- 2 teaspoons of parsley, chopped
- ½ teaspoon of chili pepper

Instructions:

Slice the chicken breasts into slices.

Add the salt, dash of black pepper, Hungarian paprika, chopped parsley and chili pepper into a large Ziploc bag. Stir well to mix. Add in the chicken slices and toss to coat.

Place the chicken breasts onto a large baking sheet and place into the freeze to chill for 10 to 15 minutes.

Preheat the oven to 350 degrees F.

Place the chicken into the oven to bake for 20 minutes.

Remove and serve immediately.

6. Spinach and Artichoke Dip

This classic dish is typically served during special events as a tasty appetizer. Best served with bread for dipping or tortillas chips.

Serving Size: 6

Cooking Time: 30 minutes

Ingredients:

- 14 ounce jar of artichoke hearts
- 12 ounce pack of frozen spinach
- 2 cups of sour cream
- 4 cups of mayonnaise
- ¼ cup of cream cheese
- 1 clove of garlic, pressed
- 1 tablespoon of crushed Aleppo pepper
- 2 ounces of grated Parmesan cheese
- 2 ounces of grated mozzarella cheese

Instructions:

Preheat the oven to 350 degrees F.

In a large bowl, add in all of the ingredients except for half of the parmesan and mozzarella cheese.

Pour the mixture into a huge baking dish. Top off with the remaining parmesan and mozzarella cheese.

Place into the oven to bake for 25 minutes.

Turn the oven to broil. Broil the dip for 5 minutes.

Remove and serve immediately with chips or bread.

7. Barbecue Pulled Chicken Sandwiches

These tiny sliders are perfect to serve during your next barbecue or during your next dinner party as an appetizer.

Serving Size: 8 to 10

Cooking Time: 6 hours and 10 minutes

Ingredients:

- 3 - 4 chicken breasts, boneless and skinless
- 1 cup of barbecue sauce
- 1/3 cup of Italian dressing
- 2 tablespoons of light brown sugar
- 1 tablespoon of Worcestershire sauce
- 2 tablespoons of cornstarch
- 2 tablespoons of water
- 8 to 10 pieces slider rolls
- Onions, for topping (qty. as desired)
- Barbecue sauce (qty. as needed)

Instructions:

Place the chicken breasts into a large slow cooker.

In a medium bowl, add in the barbecue sauce, dressing, brown sugar and Worcestershire sauce. Whisk until evenly mixed. Pour this mixture over the chicken breast. Toss the chicken to coat all sides.

Cover then cook on the lowest setting for 4 ½ hours.

Remove the chicken from the slow cooker. Shred finely with two forks.

Add the cornstarch into the slow cooker and stir well until evenly incorporated.

Cover and cook on the highest setting for 10 minutes or until the sauce is thick in consistency.

Bring the chicken into the slow cooker and toss well to mix.

Cover and continue to cook on the lowest setting for 45 minutes.

Pour some of the chicken on top of the slider rolls. Pour extra barbecue sauce over the top and serve.

8. Easy Fried Chicken

Fried chicken is a classic Southern dish but it is enjoyed all over the country. This particular recipe is very simple to prepare but it yields perfectly crispy fried chicken every time.

Serving Size: 6

Cooking Time: 45 minutes

Ingredients:

- 1 (3-pound) roaster chicken, cut into pieces
- 1 ½ cups all-purpose flour
- 2 teaspoons salt
- 1 teaspoon black pepper
- 1 cup buttermilk
- Canola oil, as needed

Instructions:

Rinse the chicken in cool water then pat dry with a paper towel.

Combine the flour, salt & pepper in a large mixing bowl.

Dredge the chicken pieces in your flour mixture then set aside for 10 to 15 minutes.

Pour the buttermilk into a bowl then dip the chicken in it then dredge it in the flour a second time.

Heat 4 inches of oil in a heavy stockpot over medium heat until it reaches 360°F.

Place the chicken pieces one at a time and fry for 10 to 20 minutes until golden brown.

Drain the chicken using paper towels and serve hot.

9. Texas Beef Brisket

If there is one thing that Texas is well known for, it is the beef brisket they are renowned for. While it may take a few hours to make, it is well worth the effort in the end.

Serving Size: 10

Cooking Time: 4 hours and 10 minutes

Ingredients:

- 2 tablespoons of powdered chili
- 2 tablespoons of salt
- 1 tablespoon of powdered garlic
- 1 tablespoon of powdered onion
- 1 tablespoon of black pepper
- 1 tablespoon of white sugar
- 2 teaspoons of dried mustard
- 1 bay leaf, crushed
- 4 ounces of beef brisket, trimmed of fat
- 1 ½ cups of beef stock

Instructions:

Preheat the oven to 350 degrees F.

In a small bowl, add in the powdered chili, dash of salt, powdered garlic, powdered onion, dash of black pepper, white sugar, dried mustard and crushed bay leaf. Stir well to mix.

Season the beef brisket with the seasoning mixture. Place into a large roasting pan.

Bring into the oven to roast for 1 hour.

Pour in the beef stock and enough water to fill ½ an inch of the roasting pan.

Reduce the temperature of your oven to 300 degrees F. Cover the roasting pan using a sheet of aluminum foil. Continue to roast for 3 hours or until the beef brisket is soft.

Remove and set the brisket aside to rest for 15 minutes before serving.

10. Apple Spiced Pork Chops with Raisins

These are the perfect pork chops to serve whenever you are craving something sweet. It is the perfect dish to make to bring in the New Year in a sweet and filling way.

Serving Size: 4

Cooking Time: 2 hours and 50 minutes

Ingredients:

- 1 gallon of water
- 1 cup of light brown sugar
- 1 cup of sea salt
- 1 cup of apple juice concentrate, frozen and thawed
- 1 ½ teaspoon of whole black peppercorns
- 2 thyme sprigs
- 4 (6-ounce each) pork chops, bone in
- Dash of sea salt
- Dash of black pepper
- Extra virgin olive oil, as needed
- For the apples and raisins:
- 2 tablespoons of unsalted butter
- 3 Granny smith apples, peeled & sliced into wedges
- 2 thyme sprigs
- ¼ cup of golden raisins
- ¾ cup of apple juice concentrate, frozen and thawed
- 3 tablespoons of light brown sugar
- ¼ teaspoon of ground cinnamon
- ¼ teaspoon of ground cloves
- Pinch of dry mustard
- Dash of sea salt
- Dash of black pepper
- ½ of a lemon

Instructions:

Preheat the oven to 350 degrees F.

In a medium bowl, add in the water, light brown sugar, dash of sea salt, thawed apple juice concentrate, whole black peppercorns and thyme sprigs. Stir well to mix. Pour this mixture into a huge Ziploc bag. Add in the pork chops and seal the bag. Place into the fridge to marinate for 2 hours.

Remove the pork chops and pat dry with a few paper towels. Season both sides using a dash of salt and black pepper.

Place a huge skillet over medium to high heat. Place in a splash of extra virgin olive oil. Once hot, add in the pork chops. Cook for 5 minutes on each side or until browned.

Transfer the pork chips into a large baking dish. Bring into the oven to bake for 30 minutes. Remove and set aside to rest.

Place a separate large skillet over low to medium heat. Place in the butter and once melted, add in the apples and thyme sprigs. Stir to coat and cook for 8 to 10 minutes.

Add in the golden raisins and the thawed apple juice concentrate. Deglaze the bottom of the skillet.

Add in the light brown sugar, ground cinnamon, ground cloves and pinch of dry mustard. Season using a dash of salt and black pepper. Squeeze your fresh lemon juice over the top and stir well to mix.

Allow to simmer for 10 minutes or until the apples are soft. Remove from heat.

Spoon the apple mixture over the cooked pork chops. Serve.

11. Cheeseburger and Bacon Pie

If you don't have to worry about the number of calories you take in and want something truly delicious, then this is the perfect dish for you to make.

Serving Size: 4

Cooking Time: 1 hour and 10 minutes

Ingredients:

- 1 tablespoon of extra virgin olive oil
- 1 onion, chopped
- 2 cloves of garlic, minced
- 1 pound of lean ground beef
- Dash of salt
- 1 tablespoon of Worcestershire sauce
- 2 tablespoons of dill pickles, chopped
- 1 teaspoon of pickle juice
- 1 tablespoon of Dijon mustard
- 1 (9-inch) pie crust, premade
- 1 cup of whole milk
- 1 egg, large
- 1 cup of cheddar cheese, shredded
- 8 strips of bacon
- Dash of black pepper

Instructions:

Preheat the oven to 350 degrees F.

Place a large skillet over medium heat. Place in the onion and cook for 5 minutes or until soft. Add in the garlic then continue to cook for an additional minute.

Add in the ground beef. Cook for 5 to 10 minutes or until the beef is browned. Remove from heat.

Add in the Worcestershire sauce, chopped dill pickles, pickle juice, Dash of salt and Dijon mustard. Stir well until evenly incorporated.

Line a large pie plate with the premade pie crust. Pour the beef mixture into the crust.

In a small bowl, add in the whole milk and large egg. Whisk to mix and pour over the beef mixture. Top off with the shredded cheddar cheese.

Place four strips of bacon over the top of the pie. Place for slices of bacon in the opposite direction over the previous slices. Season with a dash of black pepper.

Cover with a sheet of aluminum foil. Place into the oven to bake for 35 minutes.

Remove then set aside to cool for 10 minutes before serving.

12. Fried Chicken Waffles

Crispy, crunchy, sweet, and savory? This is the epitome of an American dish! These fried chicken waffles are the perfect appetizer for a large party.

Serving Size: 24

Cooking Time: 40 minutes

Ingredients:

For chicken:

- Canola oil and for frying (qty. as needed)
- 1 ¼ cups of all-purpose flour
- 2 tablespoons of cornstarch
- 1 teaspoon of cayenne pepper
- 1 tablespoon of dried Italian seasoning
- 2 teaspoons of salt
- 1 teaspoon of black pepper
- 1 cup of buttermilk
- 1 ½ pounds chicken tenders, cut into small pieces
- Hot sauce, for serving (qty. as desired)

For Waffles:

- 2 teaspoons of yeast
- ½ cup of warm water
- 1 ¾ cup of whole milk
- 6 tablespoons of butter, melted
- 2 eggs
- ½ teaspoon of pure vanilla
- 2 cups of all-purpose flour
- 1 tablespoon of white sugar
- Dash of salt
- Dash of cinnamon powder

Waffle Topping:

- 1 cup sugar
- 2 tablespoons powdered cinnamon

Instructions:

Prepare the waffles. In your bowl, combine yeast and warm water. Stir well to mix. Set aside to rest for 5 minutes or foamy.

In a separate bowl, add in the whole milk, melted butter, eggs and pure vanilla. Whisk light to mix. Add into the yeast mix.

In a different bowl, add flour, white sugar, dash of salt and powdered cinnamon. Stir to mix. Add into the milk mixture. Whisk well until smooth in consistency.

Cover and chill overnight.

Preheat a waffle iron. Grease with cooking spray.

Pour ¼ cup of the waffle batter onto the iron. Close the lid and cook for 5 minutes or until golden. Remove and repeat.

In a bowl, add in the cinnamon and white sugar for the topping. Stir well to mix. Toss the waffles with the topping until coated on all sides. Place onto a wire rack to rest.

In a pot on med heat, add 3 inches of canola oil. Heat the oil 'til it reaches 350 degrees F.

Prepare the chicken. In a bowl, add the flour, cayenne pepper, dried Italian seasoning, cornstarch, dash of salt and black pepper. Stir well to mix. In a separate bowl, add the buttermilk.

Toss the chicken in the flour mix until coated on all sides. Dip into the buttermilk and roll again in the flour mix.

Drop the chicken into the hot oil. Fry for 5 minutes or until golden. Remove and transfer onto a plate lined with paper towels.

Serve the chicken with the waffles and a drizzle of hot sauce.

13. Kale Slaw with Hazelnut Dressing

Nobody loves Kale the way Americans do! This is a delicious combination of kale, kohlrabi, hazelnuts and fruit that is rich, buttery, sweet and fresh.

Serving Size: 6

Cooking Time: 15 to 20 minutes

Ingredients:

- 1 medium kohlrabi, peeled and shredded (about 1 cup)
- 1/4 teaspoon plus 1/8 teaspoon sea salt, divided
- 6 cups kale (about 1/2 bunch)
- 1/3 cup whole hazelnuts
- 2 tablespoons cider vinegar
- 1 teaspoon grated orange zest
- 1 teaspoon grainy mustard
- 2 teaspoons fresh thyme
- 1 clove garlic, minced
- 1/4 teaspoon freshly ground black pepper
- 1/3 cup extra virgin olive oil
- 1 large of red or orange bell pepper, thinly sliced
- 2 medium carrots, peeled and shredded
- 2 medium apples or pears, thinly sliced
- 1/3 cup dried cranberries or cherries
- Parmesan cheese, shaved, optional (qty. as desired)

Instructions:

Place the kohlrabi in a small bowl, toss an 1/8 teaspoon of the salt then let sit 10 minutes. Drain as much water as possible and set aside.

Fold each leaf of kale in half lengthwise and slice out the center rib. Discard the ribs. Roll a stack of the leaves and slice in half lengthwise, then crosswise into very fine ribbons. Add to a large bowl.

Place the hazelnuts, cider vinegar, orange zest, mustard, thyme, garlic, remaining 1/4 tsp. olive oil, salt & pepper in your food processor or your blender container, and blend until well combined but still slightly chunky.

Toss together the kale and hazelnut dressing. With clean hands, firmly massage the greens for about 1 minute, or until tender. Add the kohlrabi, bell pepper, carrot, apple or pear, and dried cranberries or cherries to the kale, and toss to mix. Place on serving plates and garnish with shaved Parmesan if desired.

Enjoy!

14. Sriracha and Cheddar Burgers

Pin these burgers with stacked gooey cheeses in between two sriracha-seasoned beef patties to be on your next to-do lists. The burgers are very simple to do by placing the burgers on toasted hamburger buns and top with fried eggs if you desire.

Serving Size: 4

Cooking Time: 1 hour and 10 minutes

Ingredients:

- 1 pound ground beef
- 1 tablespoon sriracha
- 1 teaspoon Worcestershire sauce
- Salt
- Pepper
- 1/4 cup chopped fresh cilantro
- 2 teaspoons garlic powder
- 4 slices cheddar cheese
- 1 tablespoon butter
- Fried eggs (optional)
- 2 toasted hamburger buns

Instructions:

Combine the ground beef, sriracha, Worcestershire sauce, garlic powder, cilantro, salt and pepper. Mix with your hands until fully combined.

Shape into four balls and mold into a large patty, larger than a cheese slice.

Break into four pieces each cheese slice. Place two piles with a total of 8 cheese pieces, and stack in the middle of the beef patty. Cover the cheese with another patty, and tightly seal the edges by pinching together to keep the cheese intact during cooking. Repeat this process with the second burger.

Heat the butter in a large pan to moderate heat and cook the burgers for four minutes per side.

When done, place the burgers on the toasted hamburger buns. Top with fried egg if desired.

Serve!

15. Creamy Potato Salad

This creamy potato salad is sure to become a family favorite and it is the perfect dish to bring to your next picnic or get-together. To make this dish unique, try using purple potatoes!

Serving Size: 8 to 10

Cooking Time: 45 minutes

Ingredients:

- Water, as needed
- 2 pounds small Yukon gold potatoes, peeled
- 1 ½ cups mayonnaise
- 3 teaspoons apple cider vinegar
- 3 teaspoons Dijon mustard
- Salt and pepper to taste
- 1 cup diced celery
- ½ cup diced yellow onion
- 4 hardboiled eggs, peeled and diced

Instructions:

Fill a huge saucepan with 1 inch of water and bring it to a boil.

Add the potatoes then cover and return to a boil.

Reduce heat then simmer for 30 minutes or until the potatoes are tender then drain.

Let the potatoes cool slightly then chop them into cubes.

In your bowl, whisk together the mayonnaise, vinegar and mustard then season using salt and pepper.

Toss in the potatoes along with the celery, onion, and chopped eggs.

Chill the salad for 4 hours before serving.

16. Gooey Mac and Cheese

Macaroni and cheese is a favorite of kids everywhere but children aren't the only ones who can enjoy this gooey mac and cheese! Try it for yourself and you will see why!

Serving Size: 6

Cooking Time: 25 minutes

Ingredients:

- 1 pound uncooked pasta (shells or elbows)
- 1 ½ cups whole milk, divided
- 2 tablespoons all-purpose flour
- 3 cups shredded cheddar cheese (or a mixture of cheeses)

Salt and white pepper to taste

Instructions:

To get started, place a generously sized pot of water on the stove and heat it 'til it reaches a rolling boil. Add a pinch of salt to the water, and then gently add the pasta, making sure it is fully immersed in the boiling water.

Let the pasta cook for approximately 7 to 8 minutes until it reaches the desired al dente texture. Once done, drain the pasta and set it aside.

Warm 1 cup of milk in a large saucepan over medium heat – do not boil.

Stir in the flour and the remaining milk, whisking until smooth.

Keep cooking the mixture 'til it starts to thicken, stirring often – about 4 minutes.

Reduce the heat to low and stir in handfuls of cheese.

Add salt and white pepper according to your taste preferences, and then remove the mixture from heat once everything is fully melted.

Stir in the pasta until evenly coated. Serve hot.

17. Chicken Chimichangas

These delicious chimichangas are packed full of chicken, beans and rice to make a dish that is nearly impossible to resist.

Serving Size: 6

Cooking Time: 45 minutes

Ingredients:

- 1 ½ cups of chicken broth
- 1 cup of long grain rice
- ½ cup of red enchilada sauce
- 1 ½ of an onion, chopped and evenly divided
- 6 (12-inch) flour tortillas
- 4 cups of chicken breasts, cooked, chopped and evenly divided
- 1 pound of Monterey jack cheese, shredded and evenly divided
- 6 ounces can of black olives, thinly sliced
- 4 cups of refried beans, evenly divided
- ¼ cup of vegetable oil

For the topping:

- 3 avocados, peeled and pits removed
- ½ cup of cilantro, chopped
- 2 tablespoons of lemon juice
- 4 green onions, chopped
- ¼ cup of jalapeno chili peppers, chopped
- 1 tomato, chopped
- 2 cups of lettuce, shredded
- 1 cup of sour cream
- 2 cups of cheddar cheese, shredded

Instructions:

In your saucepan set over medium heat, add in the chicken broth, long grain rice and one of the chopped onions. Stir well to mix and bring the mix to a boil. Lower the heat to low. Cook for 20 minutes or until the rice is soft.

In a skillet set over low heat, add in the tortillas. Cook for 10 seconds or until warm. Transfer onto a plate and set aside.

On each of the tortillas, add the cooked chicken, shredded Monterey jack cheese, remaining chopped onion, sliced olives, cooked rice and refried beans. Roll the tortillas around the filling. Tuck the sides underneath.

In your skillet set over medium heat, add in the rolled tortillas. Cook for 3 minutes or until browned on all sides. Transfer onto a plate and set aside.

In a bowl, add in the avocado, chopped cilantro, lemon juice, chopped green onions, chopped jalapenos and chopped tomatoes. Mash well until smooth in consistency.

In a serving bowl, add the shredded lettuce. Place the chimichangas over the lettuce. Top off with the avocado mix, sour cream and shredded cheese.

Serve.

18. Chicken Noodle Soup

Whether you have a cold or you just want some tasty chicken noodle soup, this is the recipe you need. This recipe is very simple to prepare – you can be sipping soup in about 30 minutes!

Serving Size: 6 to 8

Cooking Time: 25 minutes

Ingredients:

- 1 tablespoon olive oil
- 1 medium yellow onion, chopped
- 2 large carrots, peeled and diced
- 1 tablespoon minced garlic
- 3 to 4 cups cooked chicken, cut into chunks
- 3 to 4 cups uncooked egg noodles
- ½ cup sliced green onion
- 10 cups chicken broth
- Salt and pepper to taste
- 1 teaspoon fresh chopped tarragon
- 1 bay leaf

Instructions:

Heat the oil in a huge saucepan over medium heat.

Add the onion, carrots and garlic then cook for 4 to 5 minutes until tender.

Stir in the chicken, noodles and green onion along with the chicken broth.

Season using salt and pepper to taste then add the tarragon and bay leaf.

Cover then bring to a boil then reduce heat and simmer for 10 minutes.

Discard the bay leaf then serve hot.

19. Tuna Noodle Casserole

If you are in the mood for a hot and hearty meal but don't have a lot of time on your hands, this tuna noodle casserole is the perfect solution.

Serving Size: 4 to 6

Cooking Time: 40 minutes

Ingredients:

- 1 (10.75-ounce) can condensed cream of mushroom soup
- ½ cup nonfat milk
- 2 cups cooked egg noodles
- 2 (6-ounce) cans tuna in water, drained and flaked
- 1 cup frozen peas, thawed
- ¼ cup panko breadcrumbs
- 1 tablespoon melted butter

Instructions:

Preheat the oven to 400 deg. F and lightly grease a glass baking dish.

Combine the soup and milk in a mixing bowl then toss in the noodles, tuna, and peas.

Spread the mixture in the baking dish.

Bake for 20 minutes 'til hot and bubbling then stir well.

Combine the breadcrumbs and melted butter in your bowl, and then evenly spread this mixture over the noodle mixture.

Bake for another 5 minutes or so until the crumbs are browned.

20. Apple Pecan Chicken Salad

The perfect blend of tender chicken, tart apples, and crunchy pecans, this apple pecan chicken salad is sure to become the next family favorite. Try it to see why!

Serving Size: 8 to 10

Cooking Time: 15 minutes

Ingredients:

- ¾ cups plain nonfat Greek yogurt
- 1/3 cup mayonnaise
- 2 tablespoons lemon juice
- 1 tablespoon Dijon mustard
- 4 (6-ounce each) chicken breasts, cooked and shredded
- 2 medium apples, peeled and diced
- ½ cup chopped pecans
- ½ cup diced celery
- ½ cup diced red onion
- Salt and pepper to taste

Instructions:

Whisk together the yogurt, mayonnaise, lemon juice and mustard in a large bowl.

Toss in the shredded chicken, apple, grapes, pecans, celery and red onion.

Season using salt and pepper to taste then chill until ready to serve.

21. Twice Baked Potatoes

Baked not once but twice, these twice baked potatoes are the perfect side dish for a nice grilled steak or pork tenderloin. Don't be afraid to load them up with cheese and bacon bits!

Serving Size: 4 to 8

Cooking Time: 1 hour and 30 minutes

Ingredients:

- 4 large russet potatoes, scrubbed clean
- ½ cup nonfat milk
- Salt and pepper to taste
- ¼ cup unsalted butter, softened
- 1 cup shredded cheese (plus extra)
- 2 to 3 tablespoons bacon bits

Instructions:

Preheat the oven to 375°F.

Pierce the potatoes with a fork several times then bake for 1 hour or so until tender.

Let the potatoes cool a little until you can handle them then cut in half lengthwise.

Scoop the flesh out of the potatoes into your bowl, leaving a little bit of a shell.

Mash the potatoes with a fork then stir in the milk then season using salt and pepper.

Stir in the butter and beat until light and fluffy then stir in the cheese.

Spoon the mashed potatoes into the shells and top with extra cheese and bacon bits.

Bake for 20 minutes until the top is browned and the cheese melted.

22. Southern Buttermilk Cornbread

If you are hosting a southern dinner in your home, this is one of the best dishes that you can make to accompany your meal. One bite and you will never want to buy store-bought cornbread ever again.

Serving Size: 9

Cooking Time: 55 minutes

Ingredients:

- ½ cup of butter
- 2/3 cup of white sugar
- 2 eggs
- 1 cup of buttermilk
- ½ teaspoons of baker's style baking soda
- 1 cup of cornmeal
- 1 cup of white flour
- ½ teaspoons of salt

Instructions:

Preheat the oven to 375 deg. F. Grease a baking dish with cooking spray.

In your skillet set over medium heat, add in the butter. Once melted, remove immediately from heat. Add in the white sugar. Stir well to mix. Add in the eggs and whisk well to mix.

Add in the buttermilk, cornmeal, white flour, dash of salt and baking soda. Stir well until smooth in consistency.

Pour into the baking dish.

Place into the oven to bake for 30 to 40 minutes or until baked through.

Remove and serve immediately.

23. Oklahoma Beef Brisket

This is an easy and absolutely delicious beef brisket dish you can make that will impress your friends and family. Serve with baked beans and cornbread for an authentic Oklahoman experience.

Serving Size: 8

Cooking Time: 4 hours and 30 minutes

Ingredients:

- ½ cup of honey
- 3 tablespoons of soy sauce
- Dash of seasoned salt
- 5 pound beef brisket
- 1 cup of apple cider
- ¾ cup of ketchup
- ¼ cup of light brown sugar
- 2 tablespoons of Worcestershire sauce
- ¼ cup of apple cider vinegar
- ½ teaspoons of powdered garlic

Instructions:

Preheat the oven to 300 deg. F.

Season the beef brisket with the seasoned salt and place into your roasting pan. Pour the apple cider over the brisk. Cover with a sheet of aluminum foil.

Place into the oven to roast for 3 hours.

Preheat an outdoor grill to low heat.

In a bowl, add in the honey and soy sauce. Season with a dash of seasoned salt.

Transfer the brisket on the grill. Grill for 30 minutes, basting frequently with the sauce.

In a saucepan set over low heat, add in the ketchup, light brown sugar, Worcestershire sauce, apple cider vinegar, dash of seasoned salt and powdered garlic. Whisk well until smooth in consistency. Cook for 15 minutes at a simmer.

Let the brisket rest for 10 minutes. Slice and serve with the barbecue sauce.

24. New Mexican Fish Tacos

One bite of these fish tacos and you will never want to enjoy traditional tacos ever again. These are perfect for the seafood lovers in your home.

Serving Size: 8

Cooking Time: 1 hour

Ingredients:

- 1 cup of white flour
- 2 tablespoons of cornstarch
- 1 teaspoon of baker's style baking powder
- ½ teaspoon of salt
- 1 egg, beaten
- 1 cup of beer
- ½ cup of plain yogurt
- ½ cup of mayonnaise
- 1 lime, juice only
- 1 jalapeno pepper, mined
- 1 teaspoon of capers, minced
- ½ teaspoon of dried oregano
- ½ teaspoon of powdered cumin
- ½ teaspoon of dried dill weed
- 1 teaspoon of cayenne pepper
- 1 quart of vegetable oil, for frying
- 1 pound of cod fillets, cut into 3 portions
- 12 ounces pack of corn tortillas
- ½ of a head of cabbage, shredded

Instructions:

In a bowl, add in the white flour, cornstarch, dash of salt and baker's style baking powder. Stir well to mix. Add in the beaten egg and beer. Stir well to incorporate.

In a separate bowl, add in the yogurt and mayonnaise. Add in the lime juice then stir well until smooth in consistency. Add in the minced jalapeno pepper, minced capers, dried oregano, powdered cumin, dried dill weed and cayenne pepper. Stir well to mix.

In a pot set over medium to high heat, add in the vegetable oil. Preheat the oil to 375 degrees F.

Coat the cod fillets lightly with flour. Dip into the beer mix and drop immediately into the hot oil. Fry for 5 minutes or until golden. Remove and drain on paper towels.

Serve the cod fillets onto the tortillas. Top off with the shredded cabbage. Drizzle the white sauce over the top.

Serve immediately.

25. Buffalo Chicken Pizza

This is a delicious pizza dish that is packed with a buffalo wing flavor everybody will fall in love with. It is great to enjoy for your next pizza night.

Serving Size: 6

Cooking Time: 1 hour

Ingredients:

- 3 (6-ounce each) chicken breasts, skinless, boneless, cooked and cut into small cubes
- 2 tablespoons of butter, melted
- 2 ounces bottle of hot sauce
- 8 ounces bottle of blue cheese salad dressing
- 1 (16-inch) prepare pizza crust
- 8 ounce pack of mozzarella cheese, shredded

Instructions:

Preheat the oven to 425 degrees F.

In a bowl, add in the cooked chicken cubes, melted butter and a bottle of hot sauce. Stir well to mix.

Spread the blue cheese salad dressing over the pizza crust. Top off with the cooked chicken mix.

Pour the shredded mozzarella cheese over the top.

Place into the oven to bake for 5 to 10 minutes or 'til the crust is golden.

Remove and serve immediately.

26. Blueberry Cobbler

During the summer and fall there is no better way to use fresh blueberries than in a tasty blueberry cobbler. Throw this recipe together in just a few minutes then enjoy a lovely dessert!

Serving Size: 6 to 8

Cooking Time: 55 minutes

Ingredients:

- ¾ cup unsalted butter, melted
- 2 ½ cups baking mix
- 1 cup white granulated sugar
- 1 1/3 cups nonfat milk or buttermilk
- 5 to 6 cups fresh blueberries, rinsed well

Instructions:

Preheat the oven to 350 deg. F then grease a 9x13-inch rectangular glass baking dish with cooking spray.

Melt the butter in your microwave then pour it into the dish.

Combine your baking mix and sugar in a mixing bowl then stir in the milk.

Transfer the mixture into your baking dish then sprinkle in the blueberries.

Bake for 40 to 45 minutes until the cobbler is golden brown. Serve warm.

27. White Sheet Cake

This is the perfect cake dish to make whenever you need to celebrate a special occasion. You can make this cake a day ahead of time to save yourself on time.

Serving Size: 24

Cooking Time: 40 minutes

Ingredients:

- 1 cup of butter
- 1 cup of water
- 2 cups of white flour
- 2 cups of white sugar
- 2 eggs, beaten
- ½ cup of sour cream
- 1 teaspoon of almond extract
- ½ teaspoon of salt
- 1 teaspoon of baker's style baking soda

For the frosting:

- ½ cup of butter
- ¼ cup of whole milk
- 4 ½ cups of powdered sugar
- ½ teaspoon of pure almond
- 1 cup of pecans, chopped

Instructions:

Preheat the oven to 375 degrees F.

In your saucepan set over medium heat, add in 1 cup of butter then 1 cup of water. Allow to come to a boil. Remove from heat.

Add in the white flour, white sugar, eggs, sour cream, 1 teaspoon of almond extract, dash of salt and baker's style baking soda. Whisk until smooth in consistency.

Pour into a small baking dish. Place into the oven to bake for 20 to 25 minutes or until baked through. Remove and set aside to cool for 20 minutes.

Prepare the frosting. In your saucepan set over medium heat, add in the butter, whole milk, white sugar and almond extract. Whisk well until smooth in consistency. Remove from heat. Place in the pecans and fold gently to incorporate.

Spread the frosting over the top of the cake. Serve.

28. Fudgy Chocolate Brownies

Nothing is more decadent than a moist, fudgy brownie fresh from the oven. These fudgy chocolate brownies are loaded with chocolate but feel free to add chocolate chips if you like!

Serving Size: 12 to 16

Cooking Time: 45 minutes

Ingredients:

- 1 (4-ounce) stick unsalted butter, room temperature
- 8 ounces semisweet chocolate chips, divided
- ¾ cup white granulated sugar
- 1 teaspoon vanilla extract
- 2 large eggs, whisked well
- ¾ cups all-purpose flour
- 1 ½ tablespoons unsweetened cocoa powder
- ¼ teaspoon salt
- ¼ teaspoon baking powder

Instructions:

Preheat the oven to 350 deg. F then grease and flour a square baking dish.

Melt the butter with half of the chocolate chips in your double boiler over low heat.

Stir the mixture until smooth then remove from heat and cool for a few minutes.

Whisk in the sugar & vanilla extract then add the eggs one at a time.

Combine the cocoa powder, flour, baking powder and salt in a separate bowl.

Stir the dry ingredients into your wet mixture until smooth and well combined – fold in the remaining chocolate chips.

Spread the batter in your prepared pan then bake for 25 to 30 minutes until set.

29. Easy Apple Pie

Apple pie is the quintessential American dessert and everybody loves it. This recipe for apple pie is incredibly simple to put together so try it out for your next picnic or family gathering.

Serving Size: 8 to 10

Cooking Time: 1 hour

Ingredients:

- 2 (9-inch) refrigerated pie crusts
- 1 teaspoon ground cinnamon
- 6 Granny Smith apples, medium size, peeled and sliced thin
- ¾ cups white granulated sugar
- 2 tablespoons all-purpose flour
- 2 teaspoons lemon juice
- ¼ teaspoon ground nutmeg
- Pinch salt

Instructions:

Preheat the oven to 425°F.

Place one refrigerated pie crust in a glass pie plate and gently press it against the glass.

In a mixing bowl, mix the apple slices with the sugar and flour until well combined.

Toss in the cinnamon, nutmeg, and salt along with the lemon juice.

Pour the filling into the pie plate, spreading it evenly.

Place the second crust on top of the filling and pinch together the edges of the two crusts.

Create a few small slits in the top crust, then place the pie in the oven and bake for 40 to 45 minutes 'til the crust turns a golden brown.

To avoid burning the crust edges, consider covering them with foil after the first 15 minutes of baking. This will help protect the edges while allowing the rest of the pie to continue baking to perfection.

Conclusion

This cookbook serves as a gateway to a wide array of flavors, traditions, and culinary delights that the United States has to offer.

Now, as you reach the end of this cookbook, I want to encourage you to roll up your sleeves and embark on your own culinary adventure. Don't hesitate to step into your kitchen and try out these mouthwatering recipes! Cooking is not just about nourishment; it's an art, a means of expression, and a delightful way to bring joy to yourself and your loved ones.

Whether you're a seasoned chef or just starting your journey in the culinary world, remember that mistakes are simply stepping stones to improvement. Embrace the process, have fun experimenting, and add your own personal touch to each recipe. Cooking allows you to create wonderful memories with family and friends, and you might even discover your new favorite dish along the way!

So, gather your ingredients, fire up the stove, and let the enticing aromas fill your kitchen. Let this cookbook be the starting point of many delightful meals and unforgettable experiences. As you try these recipes, you'll not only satisfy your taste buds but also gain a deeper appreciation for the diversity of American cuisine.

Wishing you happy cooking and bon appétit!

Wish You the Best

I am deeply grateful for your decision to download and read this book. It's my pleasure to share the knowledge and skills I've acquired, along with valuable tips, through the magic of writing. I trust that your experience has been both enjoyable and educational.

In a world brimming with books, I appreciate the time and thought you put into selecting mine. Your choice speaks volumes, and I'm confident that you found it to be a rewarding read.

Your honest feedback would bring me immense joy. Constructive critiques have been instrumental in my growth as an author and continue to influence my work. Your insights help me refine my content and inspire new ideas, potentially sparking the concept for my next book.

Once again, thank you for embarking on this literary journey with me.

Joris Birt

Printed in Great Britain
by Amazon

7511d6e2-ef50-4360-9927-20581735f502R01